THE DREAM
A rebus

THE DREAM

A rebus

fully illustrated by
Kim Palmer

PAGODA BOOKS

ISBN 0 946326 51 7 (hardback)

Printed in the U.K. by Hazell Watson & Viney Limited

Acknowledgements
The publishers gratefully acknowledge the kind cooporation of
Campbells and also Coca-Cola for adaptations of their tins as
featured in this book. "Coca-Cola" and "Coke" are registered
trade marks which identify the product of the Coca-Cola
Company.

INTRODUCTION

THIS BOOK IS PACKED WITH EXQUISITE ILLUSTRATIONS BUT REMARKABLY DEVOID OF TEXT. THE DREAM is in fact a modern, moral tale presented as a *rebus*★. You are therefore cordially invited to take up pen and paper and to set about solving the visual riddle that follows.

The *rebus* probably has its origin in the pictographs and hieroglyphics of old: while, of course, even today, there remains a heraldic connection, with the *rebus* widely used on coats-of-arms to spell out pictorially family names. Thus the surname 'Lockhart' might be portrayed with a key and a deer. Interestingly, too, during the sixteeth century in France, the follies of the day were often satirized in the form of a *rebus*.

There is undoubtedly a great deal of entertainment to be found in the solving of pictorial representations of the spoken word, taken syllable by syllable. In magazines earlier this century, for example, it was quite common to find a *rebus* puzzle, and this would commonly also incorporate lettering as part of the conundrum. To cite an example or two, an illustration of a taxi followed by the word 'age' might represent 'cabbage'; while a drawing of a 'soldier' with the letters 'dier' writtten beside it, but deleted, would represent 'sole'or 'soul', according to the sense of the sentence to be decoded.

In reviving the *rebus*, and presenting it here in the form of an anonymous contemporary tale, illustrated by Kim Palmer, we have opted to a rely solely on sound, allowing words and syllables to overlap at times, and also taking just the occasional liberty with pronunciation.

Punctuation is given pictorially, too, with a different representation of a stop at the end of each sentence, and an athlete representing a dash in one instance. Arrows, meanwhile, are an additional aid to following the logical sequence within each page. And, just to stretch the intellect further, one part-word in a language other than English has been included: but we believe it to be in the vocabulary of anyone able to count up to ten. You'll find, too, that we have gone for the original Latin pronunciation of 'raybus' rather than the alternative form of 'reebus'.

It is our hope  that you will find as much fun in trying to solve this *rebus* as there has been in compiling it.

★ From the Latin, meaning 'by things'.
★★Do not let a conundrum beat you.

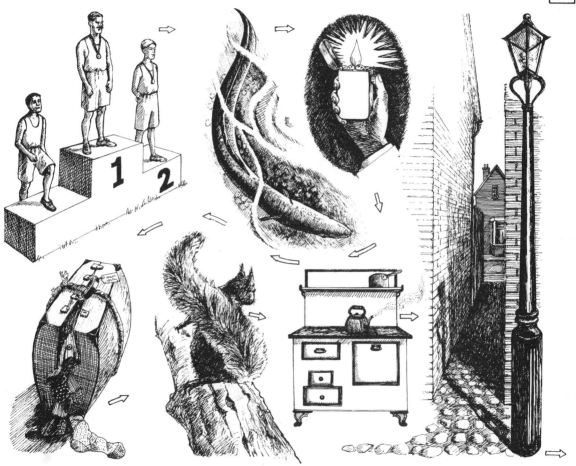

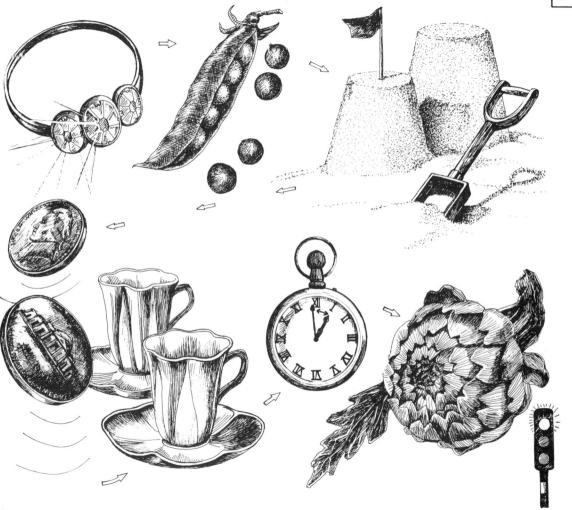

10

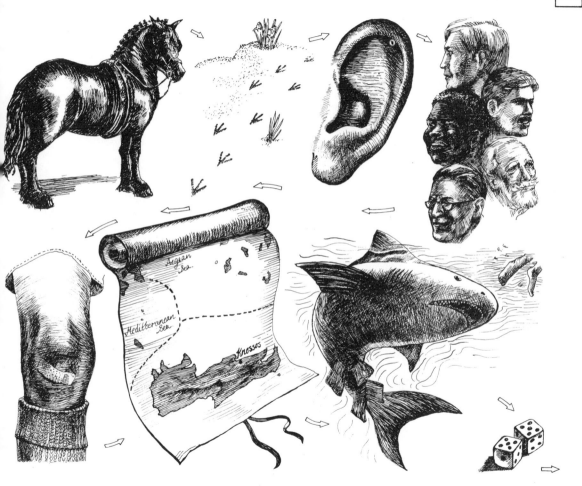

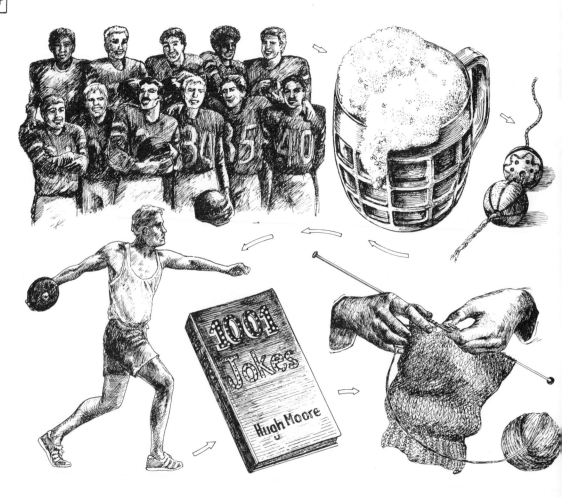

16

greater safety

BUS

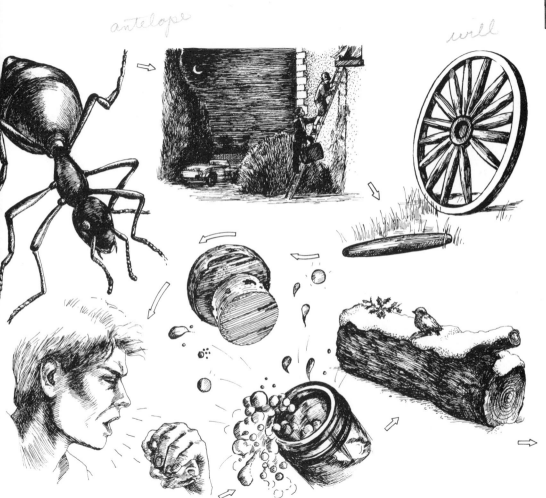

antelope

will

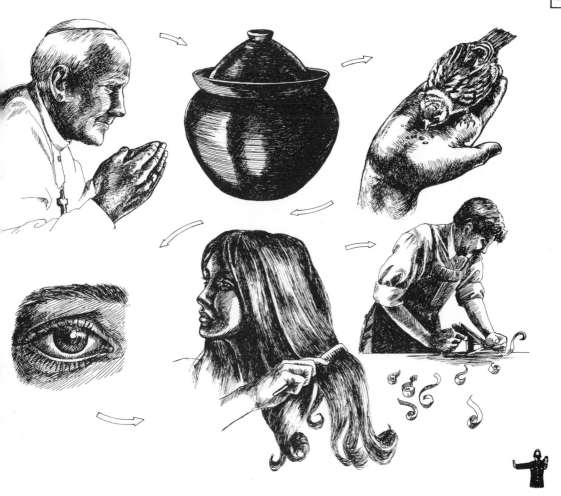

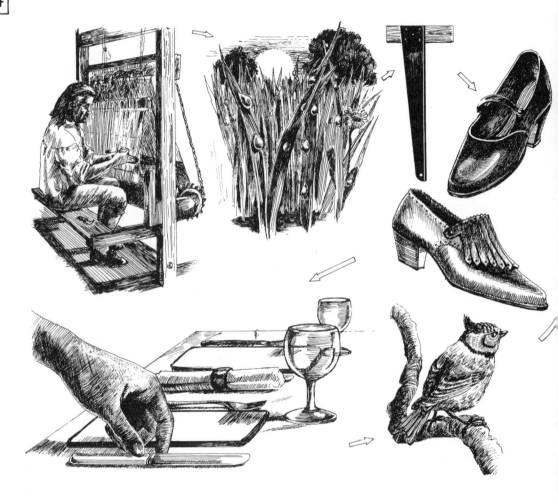

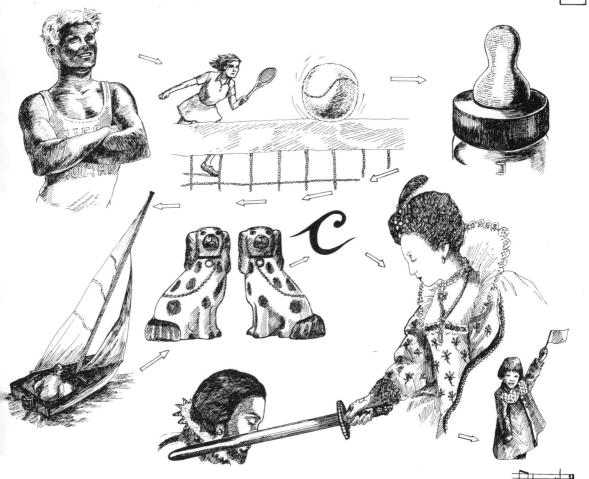

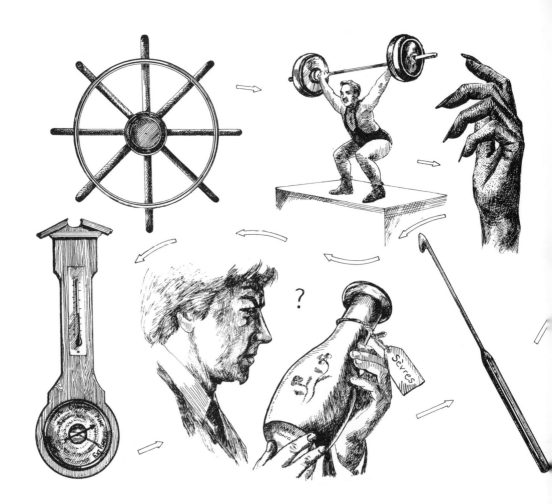

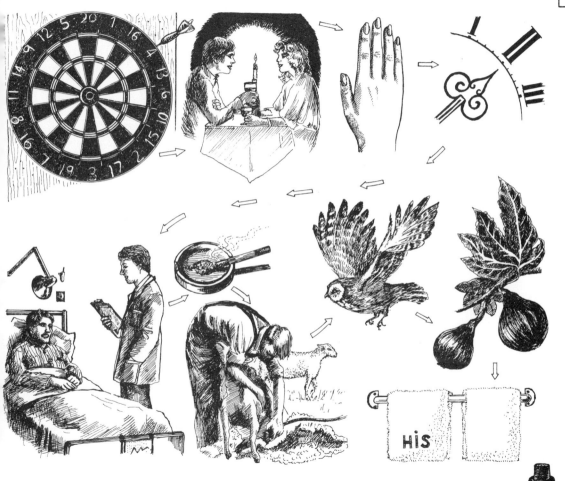

HiS

34

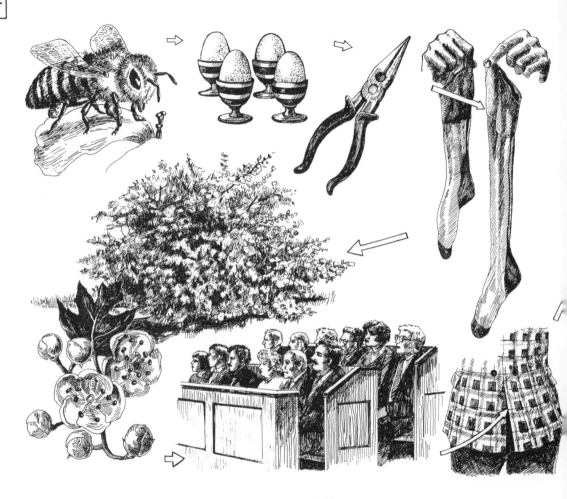

Worlds rulers

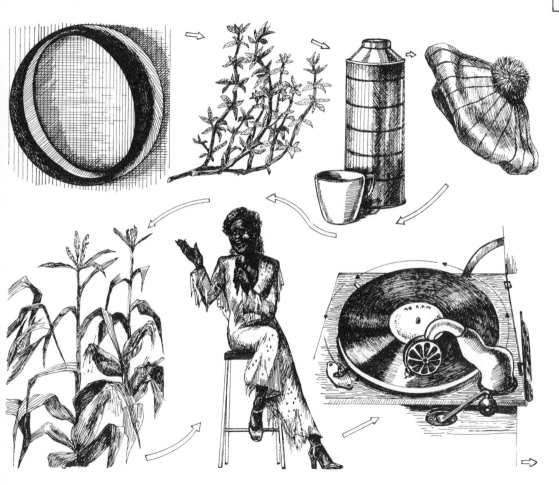

44

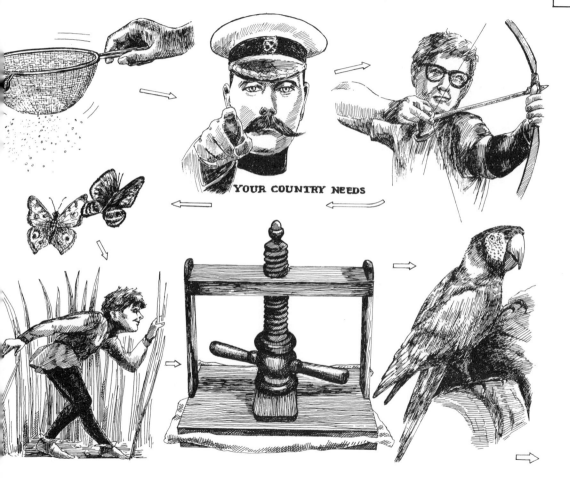

YOUR COUNTRY NEEDS

47